Let's Sort SHAPE

KIM THOMPSON

TABLE OF CONTENTS

Sight Words 2

Words to Know 3

Index 16

A Pelican Book

SEAHORSE PUBLISHING

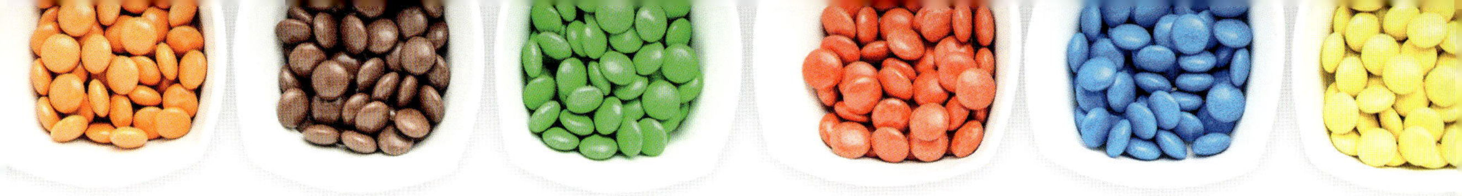

Teaching Tips for Caregivers and Teachers:

Research shows that one of the best ways for students to learn a new topic is to read about it.

Before Reading

- Read the title and predict what the book will be about.
- Read the "Words to Know" and discuss the meaning of each word.
- Read the back cover to see what the book is about.

During Reading

- When a student gets to a word that is unknown, ask them to look at the rest of the sentence to find clues to help with the meaning of the unknown word.
- Motivate students with praise and encouragement.

After Reading

- Discuss the main idea of the book.
- Ask students to give one detail that they learned in the book.

SIGHT WORDS

can
has
make
see
these
this
to
use
you

Words to Know

circles

shapes

groups

squares

rectangles

triangles

You can see **shapes**.

You can use shape to make **groups**.

groups
LIFE IS
Better
IN A
Tent
8:52

This group has **squares**.

U

This group has **circles**.

circle

This group has **rectangles.**

rectangle

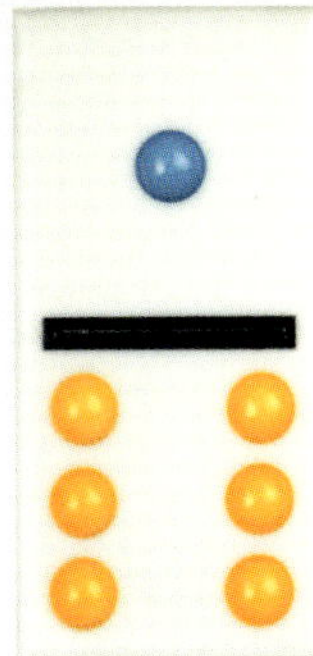

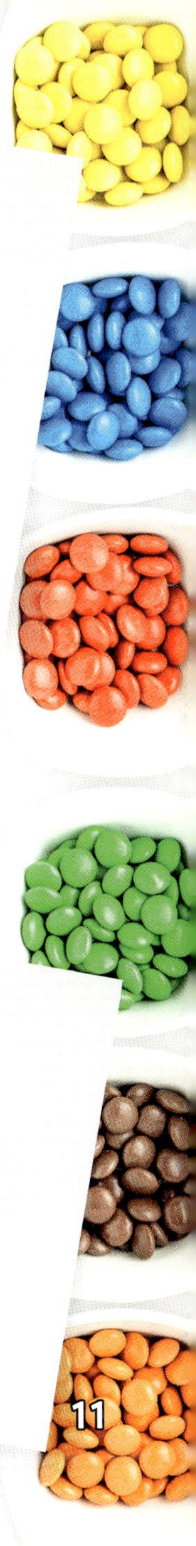

This group has **triangles**.

triangle

LIFE IS
Better
IN A
Tent

Can you group these?

Count the items on page 15.
How many groups have 5?
How many groups have 6?

U

8:52

LIFE IS
Better
IN A
Tent

Index

circle(s) 8
group(s) 4, 5, 14
shapes 4
square(s) 6
rectangle(s) 10
triangle(s) 12

Written by: Kim Thompson
Design by: Jen Bowers
Series Development: James Earley

Shutterstock.com/cover: border top ©2019 Cristina Ionescu, border bottom ©2018 3d_kot, images: ©2017 ND700, © Iurii Motov, ©2021 XELARIX, © BoxerX; p.7 ©2012 mayakova, ©2018 Janece Flippo, ©2017 4ndrei, ©2019 Jr images; p.9 ©2016 irin-k, © beboy, © Mikhail Leonov, ©2018 grey_and, ©2011 Vitaly Korovin; p.11 © Topuria Design, ©2021 Hayati Kayhan, ©2015 pics five, © Moon'D, ©2017 Africa Studio; p.13 © jekson_js, ©2015 NIPAPORN PANYACHAROEN, ©2018 Anton Starikov, ©2022 TShaKopy; p.14 ©2017 Yanas, © Chinch, © 2019 YK, © Vitezslav Valka

Library of Congress PCN Data
Shape /Kim Thompson
Let's Sort
ISBN 978-1-6389-7953-1 (hard cover)
ISBN 979-8-8873-5012-7 (paperback)
ISBN 979-8-8873-5071-4 (EPUB)
ISBN 979-8-8873-5130-8 (eBook)
Library of Congress Control Number: 2022942699

Printed in the United States of America.

Seahorse Publishing Company
www.seahorsepub.com

Published in the United States
Seahorse Publishing
PO Box 771325
Coral Springs, FL 33077

SEAHORSE
PUBLISHING